Building Self-Esteem in Girls

A Parent's Guide
to Helping Your Daughter
Develop Confidence
and Self-Esteem

by Annabelle Gilesby

Table of Contents

Introduction

A girl's self-esteem is synonymous with her sense of self-worth, self-confidence, and self-regard. Simply put, it's how she values herself. And without a doubt, helping your daughter develop self-esteem is by far the best thing that you can do for her as a parent. Adults who aren't confident in their own abilities or don't regard themselves highly rarely end up ahead in life, for example, at the top of the corporate ladder or having built meaningful relationships with others. Self-esteem plays such a vital role in a person's life, and parents should be prepared to actively participate in the building of their child's self-esteem from a young age.

Have you ever wondered why some girls seem to have a healthy self-esteem, while others don't? Would you like to the simple things you can do to instill a higher value on your daughter's sense of self-worth? In this modern world where women are given equal opportunities as men, and even a chance to surpass them, parents need to make sure that their young daughter can and will be able to compete with confidence when she grows up. Parents need to make sure that their little girl has a strong sense of self-worth, a clear self-image, and a healthy self-esteem.

Parents can only do so much for their children. Wealth and material things are great, but the best thing that parents can leave their child is a strong sense of self-worth. A young girl, especially, needs to have a healthy self-esteem so that she can fare well in society and in the world.

This book is for parents who are motivated to see their daughter grow up to be a successful and healthy person, whether as a career woman or as a loving wife and mom. Helping your daughter achieve a healthy self-esteem is absolutely the best gift you can ever give her, so don't wait another minute. Read this book and give your daughter the best gift you can give her today — a healthy self-esteem!

Chapter 1: A Parent's Role in Building Self-Esteem

What many parents don't realize is that they play a major role when children are building their self-esteem. And while it is true that the child will do most of the work, the impact of the parents on their children's lives is truly immense. Self-esteem is based on how a person sees himself. And whether parents like it or not, they and the whole family will contribute to a child's identity development. Interestingly, even when a parent is not around, he or she will have a great effect on the child's self-esteem. Therefore, parents need to be aware of the part that they play in how their child will later on see himself. Every parent must take an active step to ensure that their children have healthy perceptions of themselves.

The role of the parent in helping their child build a positive image of themselves is a crucial one. Children build their own self-esteem, and even when the parents often wish that they can do it for them, it is not possible. So, the role of parents is, basically, just to reinforce the self-esteem of their children so that they can see themselves in a positive light all the time. Does it, then, mean that orphans or those with absent parents cannot form a healthy self-esteem? They can too; however, it won't be as easy as with loving, attentive, and supportive parents. Conversely, parents need to allow their children to learn from their own experiences. They should not be too overprotective of their children, but instead teach their children useful life skills that they can apply in their lives. Furthermore, parents should not think that they can have more than the role of "reinforcer" in the building of their child's self-esteem. They should not aim to control or dictate how a child should feel about himself, or how he will create his self-identity.

The important thing that all parents need to keep in mind is that their role, when it comes to building their child's self-esteem, is to be a supporter. Every parent should take an active role in bolstering the self-confidence, self-worth, and positive self-image of their children.

Chapter 2: The Importance of Healthy Body Image

As early as five years old, children can form an unhealthy body image. Boys and girls alike can become influenced by an adult around them who has a negative body image and they can adapt this same attitude about their body and appearance. Young girls are susceptible to developing a negative body image due to the unrealistic standards of beauty set by models, actresses, singers, beauty queens, and other people that they might look up to. Mothers who are very conscious of their figures can unintentionally influence their young daughter to have an unhealthy body image.

Body image is a large contributor to self-esteem. How your daughter sees her body and how she feels about it can have a great effect on her self-worth. People form their body image based on numerous factors. Among the factors that influence body image is the unhealthy standard of beauty set by media and the society. Everywhere a young girl will look, there are size two models promoting clothes, shoes, toiletries, and other products that a young girl might want. When shopping, many clothes stores only offer garments in small sizes, causing girls to think that sizes bigger than six are not normal. Somehow it has become embarrassing to ask a saleslady for clothes in sizes ten or twelve. Society has set a standard for what body size and weight are considered normal and beautiful.

A young girl's body image can also be influenced by the people around her. Any family member who expresses a negative body image can have an impact on a girl of an impressionable age. Therefore, adults should be careful about what they say around children, especially when it concerns body weight and physical appearance. In addition, parents should always make an effort to teach their daughter to love her body no matter what size of clothes she wears. However, this should come with teaching their child the importance of practicing healthy eating habits and the benefits of exercise to the body.

How a girl forms her body image will depend on factors that influence her. Her family, teachers, classmates, and even the celebrities that she idolizes will all have an impact on her body image. So, what every parent needs to do is to teach their daughter to accept herself, to love her body no matter what, and to not allow what other people think about her weight to affect her life decisions. This is the best advice that parents can give their young daughter to help her build a healthy self-esteem.

A healthy body image is important because it affects self-esteem. It can also prevent eating disorders in young girls such as bulimia and anorexia. When parents teach their daughter early on in her life about the importance of a healthy body image, they help create a strong foundation of self-worth in her. She won't be easily affected when people comment on her weight or body size and she will be confident because she loves her body and she accepts herself.

Chapter 3: Helping Her Handle Peer Pressure

It is inevitable that children, as they grow older, will spend more and more time with their classmates and friends, rather than with their parents. Your daughter, too, will be around individuals who have values and beliefs that are very much different from what she learned in her own home. How she will handle herself around her peers will much depend on her self-esteem. Girls with a low self-esteem might not be able to handle peer pressure as effectively as those girls with a healthy sense of self-worth. Individuals with low self-confidence are usually unsure about themselves and their sense of self-worth may not be very strong. Thus, they tend to become pushovers and agree to do things that someone with a strong sense of self-worth would not normally do.

Children build their self-esteem early in their lives. They learn to value themselves based on how the parents and other family members treat them. Parents need to instill a strong sense of self-worth to their children so that they will never feel that they have to debase themselves just to please or to be accepted by other people. Peer pressure is among the biggest and scariest challenges that a young girl will face as she goes through adolescence and adulthood. There will always be that individual or group of persons that will force your child to do something that she does not want to do. However, as a parent, you don't need to worry as long as you are confident that her self-esteem is healthy and her self-worth has a strong foundation.

Moreover, parents that have taught their children good values when they were children should not be overly anxious about their child succumbing to peer pressure. The strong values that were inculcated in young children will act as their moral guide and will help them deal with every kind of situation in their life, including peer pressure. Children that have learned strong values from their parents and from the home will often use their better judgment in making tough decisions and handling difficult situations.

Socialization is very important to the development of young people. Parents need to understand that they cannot prevent their daughter from being influenced by her peers because that would be abnormal. Positive and negative peer pressure is normal and children will always be exposed to these. What parents can do is to teach their child how to react to these positive and negative peer influences. Parents can also help their daughter identify what influences are good and what among these are actually harmful for her. This is a life skill that parents need to teach their young daughter because it is not enough to teach her how to react to peer pressure. She should also be able to identify what peer influences are useful or detrimental to her. A lot of times, young people may not be able to recognize what influences are good or bad for them. Parents need to be aware of what's happening in the lives of their children, who they're hanging out with, and what activities they usually do. Although young people need to learn important life lessons by themselves, they will always benefit from the guidance of responsible and caring adults.

Peer pressure is something that every young girl will go through. With a healthy self-esteem and a solid foundation of good values, your daughter will be prepared to face every challenge that goes her way. So while the children are young, parents should teach their children good values and help them to form a habit of making wise choices, as part of the training to build a healthy self-esteem.

Chapter 4: Ten Steps to Build Her Self-Confidence

Teaching your daughter to believe in herself and in her abilities can help promote a healthy self-esteem. When she is confident about her appearance and capabilities, she can build a positive self-image. Self-confidence allows a person to push on and, therefore, accomplish goals, to try new things, and to meet new people. Confident girls were raised to believe that there is nothing they cannot accomplish with hard work and determination. Again, parents play an important role in building their child's confidence. Here is a 10-step plan that parents can follow to help build their daughter's self-confidence.

Step 1: Provide a Safe Environment

In order to build confidence, your child will need to feel that she is in a safe and stable environment. Parents need to be trustworthy and they need to be around for their daughter when she needs them for anything at all.

Step 2: Don't Expect Too Much from Your Daughter

Never pressure your daughter to achieve something that she can't. Parents need to be careful when encouraging their children to accomplish goals, because children can feel pressured, and they may do tasks not because they want to, but just to please their parents. Instead, be aware of your child's strengths and things that she can improve on. Provide the means for her to develop her skills and give her the time she needs to attain goals.

Step 3: Let Her Make Her Own Goals

Teach your child the importance of having goals. When she makes goals and she achieves these, her confidence in herself and in her abilities will grow. She will feel happy that she was able to accomplish something worthwhile. The duty of parents is to teach their child to create realistic goals and help her achieve these.

Step 4: Allow Mistakes

In fact, teach her to embrace mistakes. After all, mistakes teach valuable lessons to those that commit them. Don't be one of those parents that can't tolerate mistakes and failures. Allow mistakes to happen and be supportive of your daughter when she fails at something. Teach her that to make mistakes is but natural, and that no person on this earth is perfect. However, make her realize what she did wrong and help her identify what she can do to prevent the error on her next try.

Step 5: Praise Her for Achievements

Children need to be praised by their parents and it is the job of every mom and dad to make their child feel good about themselves. Children whose parents withhold praises or fail to recognize their child's achievements often develop self-esteem issues.

Step 6: Give Her Choices

Among the best ways to help your daughter develop self-confidence and build a healthy self-esteem is to allow her to make her own decisions. So, depending on her age, you could give her a say in some things instead of just deciding everything for her. For example, you could ask, "So, what would you like to do this summer vacation, take a music class or just stay at home and get some rest? By giving her choices, she can practice making decisions and she can also learn from the decisions she made.

Step 7: Encourage Her to Try New Things

Again, be careful about pressuring her to do things she may not be ready for. Every parent is aware of what their child is capable of, so use your parental instinct to know what things your daughter might want to try and be ready to open new doors for her.

Step 8: Avoid Negative Criticism

Young people do not respond positively to negative criticism. They will just feel sad or angry that their parents can use hurtful language towards them. Negative criticism is not effective so just don't use it on your children. Instead, opt for constructive criticism and only say things to your daughter that she can use to improve herself.

Step 9: Teach Problem Solving Skills

When your daughter has a problem that you know she can solve by herself, permit her to do so. Encourage her to open up to you about anything that's troubling her and always offer sound advice. However, you should refrain from spoon-feeding her with answers and instead allow her to arrive at possible solutions for her problem during your conversation. Lead her so that she can make the right decisions.

Step 10: Be a Positive Role Model

Perhaps one of the most difficult duties of a parent is to always be a good model for their children. Children will follow in their parents' footsteps and will imitate what they see in their parents. So if you want to teach your daughter good values, then you need to do it by example. Also, you need to have self-confidence and a healthy self-esteem if you want your daughter to have these.

Chapter 5: Identity Development

As your daughter goes through adolescence, she will find her identity and will start to develop a clearer and stronger sense of self. Parents need to help their child attain a strong identity because this is how she will see herself. When girls have a strong identity or sense of self, they become more flexible, more independent, and more confident. These are qualities that help build a healthy self-esteem.

The Importance Hobbies to Finding One's Self-Identity

Among the many benefits of having hobbies is to help your daughter develop her self-identity. Whether your child likes music, sports, or arts, having a hobby will help her have a clear sense of who she is. Hobbies can be a pastime but at the same time, it helps your child develop skills. And as your daughter continues to enjoy her hobby, her skill will grow and over time, she will become an expert. Being adept at something can boost a person's confidence and self-esteem.

A young person's self-identity can also be formed by knowing what she likes and dislikes. If she likes music and dislikes sports, then she has a clear idea of what activities make her feel happy and good about herself. She also knows what activities she'd rather not do because they neither interest her nor help improve her self-confidence. Your daughter can have a strong self-identity when she is able to find out for herself the things that she enjoys doing and the things she does not like to do. This helps her to have a clearer idea of who she is. So, while children are young, parents need to expose them to as many activities as possible.

The Role of Sports in Building Self-Esteem

The role of sports in building a child's self-esteem has long been established. Young girls who engage in sports have a healthy self-esteem. They are confident because of their skills and they are able to socialize easily with other people. Girls who join in sports activities tend to be more confident already simply by being members of a sports team.

Group sports as well as individual sports both have advantages when it comes to helping a young girl build her self-esteem. Group and individual sports allow a person to develop social skills, athletic prowess, and self-confidence. It also teaches a player values such as cooperation, healthy competition, and sportsmanship. These positive traits contribute to a healthy sense of self-worth.

Sexual Identity and Self-Esteem

Puberty is the time when a person's sexual identity develops. As a parent, you need to provide a safe and accepting environment for your daughter in order for her to form her sexual identity. It can be uncomfortable for most parents but your daughter will need to know that her parents are her supporters and not her criticizers. When children are not allowed to find their sexual identity because of fear or embarrassment, their self-esteem is affected. Parents need to be open-minded and be ready for the fact that their daughter can be a lesbian.

Allow your child to find her sexual identity because it is a part of who she is. When she is successful in doing so and she has a loving, supportive environment, then she can build a healthy self-esteem.

Chapter 6: Activities that Help Build Self-Esteem

And while it is true that a healthy self-esteem with a strong foundation is developed from a very young age and from the home, children who have low self-esteem can still improve and develop their self-confidence and gain a stronger sense of self-worth. Here are some activities that help build or improve the self-esteem.

Activity 1: Goal-Setting

This activity will help your child create and achieve goals. Teach her this goal-setting activity and she can use it every time she has goals that she needs to attain.

Step 1: Create a Goal

Ask your daughter if there is something that she would like to achieve this week. Make sure that the goal is realistic such as getting a good score in a test, finishing a project, or cleaning her room. Talk about why this goal is important to her.

Step 2: Jot It Down

Ask your daughter to write down this goal on a piece of paper. It can be a notebook page or a Post-It note. She can also have a "Goals Board" if she likes, so that she can start putting all of her future goals there.

Step 3: Put It Somewhere Visible

Tell your daughter that she should stick the paper in a place where she can easily see it. This will remind her of her goal and will keep her focused in accomplishing it.

Step 4: Create a Plan

In this next step, ask your daughter to create a plan of action. How does she plan to get a high score in the test? How can she finish her project on time? What part of her room will she start cleaning? If she likes, she can also write down on paper the steps of her plan. That way, she can remember them clearly.

Step 5: Attain Your Goal

Tell your daughter that she needs to put a deadline for her goal and that she needs to keep this deadline. Explain to her the importance of attaining a goal and not just creating it. So she should always find a way to accomplish the goals that she writes down.

Time and time again, remind your daughter to set realistic goals and not impossible ones. Your goal is to build her self-esteem and setting high and unrealistic goals can only hurt your child's self-confidence and self-worth.

Step 6: Reward Yourself

To keep your daughter motivated in achieving her goals, tell her to reward herself every time she successfully achieves a goal. You can help her out by offering the reward but you should tell her that rewards are not always monetary in nature.

Activity 2: Self-Esteem Affirmations

This activity will help your child maintain a strong sense of self-worth. Children with low self-esteem can develop a healthier self-esteem through this activity.

Step 1: Create Affirmations

Affirmations are positive thoughts that you want to enforce. Explain to your child how affirmations work and ask her to write some positive thoughts that she'd like to tell herself. Here are some examples.

"I am beautiful."

"I am loved."

"I am in a safe place."

"I am special."

"I am who I am."

"I accept myself."

Step 2: Say Your Affirmations

In this next step, ask you daughter to remember these positive thoughts and tell her that whenever she feels that she is losing her self-confidence or is feeling unsure of herself, all she needs to do is to say these sentences out loud. She can repeat them to herself as many times as she needs to, until she feels better and feels assured that she is, indeed, a special girl, and that no one or nothing can make her feel otherwise.

Activity 3: Peer Pressure Role Playing

In this activity, parents can prepare their child for situations when she will feel pressured by her friends or some other person to do something that she doesn't really want to do. In Chapter 3, peer pressure was discussed and in this activity, you and your daughter can role play situations that she could or might experience inside or outside the school campus.

Step 1: Prepare Situations

The parent and the child can talk about situations where she might experience peer pressure. Example situations:

- Bullying situations

- Asking her to smoke, drink liquor, or try drugs

- Asking her to engage in sexual activities

- Asking her to hurt someone

- Asking her to do anything that is morally wrong

- Asking her to commit a crime

Step 2: Role Playing

You and your daughter can do the role playing. You can be the friend or the person that pressures your daughter or you can play your daughter so that she can see how you would react to the peer pressure. Make sure that your daughter is comfortable with this activity before proceeding. You can also exchange roles and you can check how your daughter would react to the peer pressure. It is important that you don't give a sermon about what you think she should do.

Step 3: Learning the Lesson

As the adult, it is very easy to just tell your daughter how to react to peer pressure. You can dictate to her what she needs to do but she won't be able to learn from her experience if you do so. So during the role playing, let her show you how she would react in case she was faced with a peer-pressure situation. At this point, you can talk together about how she handled the situations and you can encourage her that her reactions were good. Nevertheless, take this chance to give your advice on how to better handle the situation.

Conclusion

A girl's self-esteem is very important because it can make her into a confident and well-adjusted woman when she grows up. It is, therefore, every parent's duty to make their daughter feel special and achieve a strong sense of self-worth.

Girls that have healthy self-esteems will grow up to be accomplished women and these women are the very ones that, ultimately, make a difference in the world either from a swivel chair in an office or from a couch in her living room.

Gone are the days when women were expected to just stay in the home to cook for her husband and to care for the children. We live in a modern world, and now more than ever, we need to produce women that can make an impact in this world. It starts with our young daughters. Helping our young girls to love and accept themselves, encouraging their interests, and providing opportunities for them to learn and develop skills are just a few things that a parent can do to help her child build a healthy self-esteem.

Finally, I'd like to thank you for purchasing this book! If you found it helpful, I'd greatly appreciate it if you'd take a moment to leave a review on Amazon. Thank you!

Made in the USA
Middletown, DE
31 August 2017